How to Search for a Pastor In Today's Church

Finding Gods Man For His Church

Scott K. Delashaw

Copyright © 2010 by Scott K. Delashaw

How To Search For A Pastor In Todays Church
Finding Gods Man For His Church
by Scott K. Delashaw

Printed in the United States of America

ISBN 9781612151298

All rights reserved solely by the author. The author guarantees all contents are original and do not infringe upon the legal rights of any other person or work. No part of this book may be reproduced in any form without the permission of the author. The views expressed in this book are not necessarily those of the publisher.

Unless otherwise indicated, Bible quotations are taken from The King James Bible.

To order additional copies e-mail us at
skdbooks@yahoo.com

www.xulonpress.com

Contents

Foreword ix

Introduction xi

Chapter 1
    Saying Goodbye to the Former Pastor .. 15

Chapter 2
    To Interim or Not to Interim? 23

Chapter 3
    Forming a Pastor Search Committee 33

Chapter 4
    Posture of the Church During
    the Search 45

Chapter 5
    Starting the Process 54

Chapter 6
    What is a Pastor? 83
Endnotes..99
Appendix...101

Dedication

To my father, Willie Delashaw for his example
and faithful years in the pastorate.
To my father-in-law, Hollis Retherford, the
pastor of the church where I met Christ.
To my former pastor, Clyde Goodlet who went
home to be with the Lord during this project.

Foreword

Numerous times throughout my ministry, God has placed individuals in my path that made an unforgettable impression on me—individuals who changed my life. Brother Scott Delashaw was one of them. Meeting him was a "God moment" for me.

In my 48 years of ministry, I have read many books, but I have never seen or read a book dealing with how to search for a pastor. As I read this manuscript, I thought of the tremendous need there was for this book which offers churches practical instruction for conducting a search for a pastor. I encourage any church leader or member of a search committee that is serious about finding the man that God wants for their church, to read this book. I pray they would read the book, and let God direct them in calling the right pastor.

Thanks Scott for taking the time to put your thoughts on paper. This book is much needed by the Church.

Rocky Goodwin
Director, Evangelistic International Ministries
Warren, Arkansas

Introduction

Recent statistics show that the typical tenure of a Baptist pastor in Alabama is a little more than 36 months.[i] This figure may be shocking to some, but seasoned pastors know this statistic to be all too true.

This is not just an issue for Baptists alone. A recent survey of evangelical organizations and mainstream denominations shows the same problem, pastors serving short tenures.[ii] It is clear to me that this is an issue around the country. There are many reasons for this, but that is not the focus of this book.

For every church without a pastor, there is a group of people appointed by that church's congregation to search for the new pastor—a search or pulpit committee. If one has never served on a committee or team assigned to find, interview, and present a prospective pastor to a church, one has no idea how hard it can be. And now such searches have become even harder.

Pastors are like snowflakes. At a distance we may all look alike, but up close we are all different in some way. The search committee must look closely, and work together harmoniously to find the right candidate. Of course that candidate should have all of the obvious skills. He must be able to preach to every maturity level in the church, appeal to the youth, stress missions, push evangelism, revive discipleship, and so on. The challenge will be searching for such a pastor prayerfully, purposefully and patiently.

For some churches, it seems like just yesterday they were calling a new pastor and *now* they are preparing to begin another search. (Search committee member could be a full time job for them!) Other churches have enjoyed a long period of time with the same pastor, so searches are rare. The members of those churches must now begin a task that few, if any, have ever performed. This book can help both churches.

As a pastor who has dealt with many search committees over the years, I have picked up many bits and pieces of information from various search committees. I've gleaned much, both from things they did that *worked well,* and things they did that *went terribly wrong.*

God placed it upon my heart to put together this project in hopes of helping churches avoid unnecessary pains and problems that develop when a search is performed poorly or improperly. *Some readers will not agree with, nor adopt everything in this book.* That is fine. But my hope is that every reader will find something that will aid and encourage them as they search for and find their next pastor.

I love the Lord's churches and am very protective of His people. It burdens me to see pain and division brought on by the search for a new pastor. Recently I spoke with a man serving as the chairman of a pulpit committee. He shared how their flawed approach to their current search has now resulted in a divided congregation, and an empty pulpit. His wife remarked that they had lived, breathed, ate, and slept with this issue for almost a year now! Brethren, I believe this can be avoided with prayer, patience, and a plan.

May God bless you as you begin your search. I pray that God uses this small book to help your church, and the right pastor, to find each other.
Brother Scott

Chapter 1

Saying Goodbye to the Former Pastor

In his play entitled *Romeo and Juliet*, Shakespeare wrote that "parting is such sweet sorrow."[iii] If we are honest, most of us could say this describes our feelings toward one or more pastors we have had in our Christian experience. Some pastors we miss a great deal. Parting from them will be sweet sorrow. On the other hand, some pastors will be missed very little. Parting from those pastors will just be sweet! Either way, there is a time when all things, good or bad, will come to an end. That is the nature of things in this world.

When your pastor resigned, he relinquished his position of leadership in your church. Therefore, it is necessary to adjust your relationship with him accordingly. Hopefully he will still be on good terms with the church and welcome if he returns for a visit. But even if he left under unfavorable conditions, a relationship still exists.

When a pastor leaves after ministering well, it is difficult to *let go* of him. If we are not very careful, we can tend to measure all future candidates against him unfavorably. On the other hand, when a pastor's tenure ends with problems and pain, we can too easily or quickly measure all future candidates favorably. This is a natural reaction but not a spiritual reaction. Either way, it is unfair to potential candidates.

God has moved the departed pastor on for a reason. If the Lord gave you a carbon copy or a clone of your former pastor—the departed pastor could still be there. The Lord's men are called and equipped by Him. But each one is very different from the other. God moves His men as He sees fit to meet the needs of His church.

For instance, one pastor may be the fiery evangelist when he preaches. He may be passionate about local and home missions. He may pastor a church for five years and baptize twenty new converts a year. But the same pastor may place little emphasis upon personal growth and discipleship. Then one day, God begins to stir in that pastor's heart and mind. Without a doubt God is moving his man to another place of service. The pastor resigns by saying "God has led me somewhere else."

Now this vibrant, growing church has many "babes in Christ" in its membership who need personal growth and steady teaching. So God moves the fiery, evangelistic pastor elsewhere and brings in a pastor with a special gift for teaching doctrine and discipline to young Christians. He moves the fiery evangelist to a church that is doctrinally deep, but evangelistically shallow.

God's purpose here is to use the giftedness of these two ministers to *declare* the gospel and to *disciple* His people. But if the search team sets out to find someone exactly like brother "Last Pastor," they may disregard brother "Next Pastor," and miss God's will completely.

I am convinced that there are churches and pastors today who, by reason of a lack of prayer and discernment, are in a relationship that is within God's permissive will, but not His perfect will.

Peter and Paul were drastically different men. Barnabas and Silas probably were too. John Mark and Timothy seem to be as different as night and day. All of these men became great men of God. But it is God who made these men who they were. He used them in very different ways to accomplish his will.

You are now searching for God's man for this hour. There are some great men of God out there, but don't accept less than the will of God for your church.

In regard to the former pastor who is resigning or retiring from your church, I say this: If you truly love the church, you must limit (at least at first) your involvement with it. If you have resigned, but are still in active ministry, move on and stay far away from any action or activity that could influence the business of the church. Your opportunity for exhorting and instructing the church has passed. Pastors should prepare the church to search for their replacement *from* the pulpit, *before* they leave.

If you are retiring from the pastorate but would like to continue attending and worshiping with them, it would be best for you to attend another church, at least for awhile. Let the church call their next pastor before you return to the congregation. Even then, you should limit your involvement in the church, excluding any activity that could be interpreted as an attempt to undermine the influence or authority of the new pastor.

I personally believe that a retired pastor, who intends to stay on as a member of the church he pastored, should meet with the new pastor to express support for him. He should assure the new pastor that, as the new pastor, he will receive the honor and respect due to him. The reasons for this are many and should be obvious so I won't take the time to list them all but let me briefly mention two of them. One, the retiring pastor can be an example to the rest of the congregation by willfully and humbly submitting to the authority and leadership of those who have the rule over him (Hebrews 13:17). Two, he will help prevent the new pastor from feeling intimidated by his presence in the church. Simply put, Moses had to yield to Joshua.

One final word to the departing pastor. Very few men are able to name their replacement without being criticized heavily, so be careful. Also, as a departing pastor, you should never try to *"get someone a church"* by using your influence.

If you receive a formal request from the search committee for information on a prospective pastor, you should limit your comments to general information, neither condemning, or recommending the candidate. **The lone exception to this rule is if you are aware of something related to a candidate that could be devastating to the church.**

Finally, someone once said "you cannot live in the past." I believe many churches today are dying in the present because they are doing just that.

Before a church can move into an exciting new chapter of life and service, they must seek out God's man who can lead them into it. The search for a pastor can be challenging and stressful. But if you find the man God has prepared to lead your church, it will be well worth it! May God bless you as you search for your next pastor.

Chapter 2

To Interim or Not to Interim? That is the First Question!

When your pastor resigns, a void is left in the pulpit. The span of time between the departing and new pastor is the "interim period." A church must decide the best way to fill the empty pulpit for Sunday and midweek services.

Some churches choose to fill pulpit responsibilities from month to month, or even week to week. These are usually smaller churches with little activity during the week. They are also usually acquainted with young preachers or retired pastors who are happy to help them out.

On the other hand, medium and large congregations may choose to divide pulpit responsibilities among the ministerial staff of the church.

Another option for churches is the *Interim Pastor*. The word *interim* means **having temporary effect;** *serving as a temporary measure until something more complete and permanent can be established.* Should a church opt to call an Interim Pastor (IP), both the IP and the calling church must be very clear on the expectations for the IP.

The IP is to be a temporary person in the life of the church. (I have a friend who once served as an IP for so long, he began to refer to himself as the "eternal interim"!) The IP is intended to free the church from worry regarding pulpit responsibilities and a few pastoral duties.

Even with an IP in place, a church must never forget the arrangement is only temporary. A church and its search committee must not become lethargic and complacent with things as they are. The search for the new pastor must remain an active priority for the church. It does not mean they should rush. It simply means that while they are wise to be patient in the search, the goal must be to avoid a protracted search.

Many times a church will begin to struggle or decline when the search for a pastor moves into multiple years. I am familiar with a church that had an IP for five years. He was not interested in leaving and they were not interested in looking. The church became essentially dormant. There was no outreach, no evangelism, no vision... just complacency. The church lost several members including a longtime leader. What a sad testimony!

Having witnessed the devastation that such a problem can cause, let me list a few suggestions that I believe will help the church that is about to call an IP.

1. Do not have the church body vote in an IP.

Any vote of the whole church body to install a person in a position will require a vote of the whole church body to remove them, if they do not voluntarily step down. (The wisdom of this will become clear as you read.)

The church should empower the deacons or a selected committee to call and to release the IP at the appropriate times. Simply prepare a motion for your next business meeting that states "they will be given the authority to act in behalf of the entire church body in respect to the calling and releasing of an Interim Pastor as they see fit".

2. Make it clear to the IP *and to the church* that, at no time, is the IP to be considered for the pastoral position. In order to avoid any misunderstanding, some churches now have IP's sign a contract to this effect. (Appendix A)

At the first sign that an IP may be garnering support for candidacy as pastor, he should be released immediately. Some may insist: "We voted in our IP and he was the best pastor we ever had." Sadly, such an experience is an extreme exception, but far from the rule. More often than not, when the IP announces his interest in the vacancy, with or without knowing it, he does two things:

First, he goes beyond the terms of his agreement with the committee that called him. If a potential IP has the intention and desire to pastor a church, he should inform the committee up front so that they may continue looking elsewhere for an interim.

Second, he undermines the work of the Pastor Search Committee (or PSC). After all, they are actively praying, reviewing resumes and interviewing prospective pastors.

What a mess it can make of a church when part of the church body wants the IP while the other part wants to honor the work of the PSC (Pastor Search Committee). This mess can cause a highly developed spirit of division among the membership that will threaten the future of the church. (I have witnessed this very scenario take place twice within the last 12 months.) This type of activity has dealt *near death blows* to churches all over the country. Just imagine the disgust that heaven must have over our careless and fleshly ways!

3. Clearly outline the duties and expectations for the IP.

He is there to preach on Sundays and at mid-week services. He may be asked to do some additional pastoral work that becomes necessary, such as conducting funerals, or hospital visits to those near death. There may be some administrative duties that need to be kept current. Whatever the responsibilities, it must be clear that he is not to be involved in any church business, or PSC business.

4. He is still to be honored because he is a man of God.

Many IPs have poured out their life in the service of our Lord in another church or ministry. He is usually a man of wisdom and full of the Holy Spirit. He should be treated with respect.

5. The IP should be released by the committee at the proper time.

It would not be a bad idea for the church to have a luncheon or a fellowship supper to show appreciation for ministry of the I.P. and his family. If he has served the church for an extended time, a gift for him and his wife would a nice way to say "thank you".

The ministry of IPs has proven valuable to countless churches through the years. It is intended to ease the pressure and urgency of calling a permanent pastor. The interim period can also be a precious time in which God can use a minister to help a church heal, or become unified after a time of hurt or division. When you prepare to call your Interim Pastor, take these simple steps (or similar steps) to ensure peace and unity within the church as you search for a pastor.

Should Our Church Call an Interim Pastor

or

Fill the Pulpit Week to Week?

Sometimes it is difficult to know whether or not to enlist the service of an Interim Pastor (IP). Here are a few questions that may help you:

1. Will you be able to fill the pulpit with a quality message each week?
2. Will you be able to fill the pulpit in advance for at least 1 month?
3. Does your church historically do well between pastors or does it typically suffer a decrease in attendance?
4. Do you think your church will have an easy time forming a Pastor Search Committee?

Important: If your answers to the questions above are "no", then you should seriously consider calling an IP.

5. Has your former pastor been with you for a long period of time, say 10 years or more?
6. Did your pastor leave suddenly (due to unforeseen circumstances)?
7. Did your pastor's term end in turmoil, leaving the church hurt, damaged or divided in a significant way?

Important: If the answers to questions 5 – 7 are "yes," you should consider calling an IP.

Chapter 3

Forming a Pastor Search Committee

One of the most serious responsibilities a person can accept from their church is to serve on a Pastor Search Committee (PSC). These folks can literally go from hero to zero overnight. Speaking as a pastor, I do not envy those who serve on such a committee. We pastors are well aware of how difficult some people are to serve, much less satisfy. Add to this the increasingly difficult job of finding a sound, gifted, passionate pastor, who is just as great when you meet him as how he looked "on paper"—you've got yourself a task.

This chapter contains the nuts and bolts of forming this most important committee.

Who Selects This Committee?

A church-wide season of prayer must be the first action taken when forming a committee. Prayer is essential to the entire search process. Choosing the individuals to serve on your committee should be conducted prayerfully and thoughtfully. For if you ask ten people how this should be done, you may get ten different answers. There are a number of ways a committee can be formed.

Some congregations simply delegate this responsibility to the deacons. *If your church is fortunate enough to have only mature, godly deacons, by all means use some of them.*

Unfortunately, it is my observation that there are a large number of men in today's church who are allowed to serve in the office of a deacon, though they are clearly not qualified to do so. Only the most qualified men available should be selected to search for a qualified pastor. Still, there is no reason why spiritually mature laymen cannot be used to serve in this capacity. This is not a "deacon only" position.

A few churches take open nominations from "the floor" and vote on them. This is just a bad idea. Too often the response of the nominated is along these lines, "Well, I'd rather not do it, but if nobody else will do it, I will." Is this really the guy you want on the forefront of the search for your next pastor? These folks may be alright for planning your next church picnic, but not for finding the next pastor to lead your church!

To put it another way, if you needed a heart transplant, would you like a person with this motivation to find you a heart and/or the best heart surgeon: "I'd rather not do this, but if nobody else will do it, I will"? Finding a new pastor is just too important a responsibility to entrust to those who will not give their best effort.

Other congregations use their nominating committee. This group of people should have a pretty good idea of the capabilities of teachers and leaders within the church. They are already charged yearly with gathering personnel to present to the church to fill many vital positions. With the same gravity of mind and spirit, they should be able to select and present to the congregation acceptable PSC candidates for approval. This seems to have become the **best** and **simplest** way of appointing members to a PSC.

If your church does not have a nominating committee already in place, and does not intend to form one, then give each eligible voting member of the congregation a blank slip of paper. Instruct them to write the names of the five people they believe are most qualified to serve on such a committee. Take up the slips and have the Chairman of Deacons tally the vote to determine the five most named (qualified) individuals. Then approach each of these people separately and discuss their willingness to serve on the Pastor Search Committee (PSC).

Who Serves on This Committee? How Many Should Serve?

Once you have determined *how* your PSC will be selected, the next step is to determine *who* these people will be and how many you will have on the committee. Provide the information below to every member of your church body. (Or provide this book to every person for their instruction.)

As to the number of people to have on this committee, I would suggest no less than three people and no more than seven. The optimum number is five. (This number should be adjusted upward for churches with 500 or more people in regular Sunday school attendance.)

An odd number prevents a tie vote and five is few enough to encourage unity. I recall one church appointing nine people, plus an alternate, to their PSC—though they averaged less than 100 people in Sunday School. This meant 10% of their church was on the committee! It is difficult enough to keep unity among 7 members, much less 10.

As to who these people will be, this is the most important step.

Please understand that what I am about to say has been gleaned from my experience dealing *with* committees and not from serving *on* them. This advice is also a cross-section of the wisdom of other pastors who have dealt with PSCs.

1) PSC members should be men. God mandates that men should be the head of the home *and* that they should be the leaders of His Church. I am immediately suspect of a church who cannot find at least three men suitable to interview a prospective pastor. If the ladies of the church are not to preach, pastor, teach men, or usurp the authority of men, then it stands to reason that the church should not put them in this position.

I assure you this is not a chauvinistic rant. It is an unpopular but scriptural truth. Some of the most faithful, hard working members of the church are women. In the church where I serve as the pastor, there are extremely dedicated and doctrinally educated women. However, they understand that God has clearly given different roles to men and women within the structure of the church. Having said that, each church is autonomous and has the privilege of selecting anyone they so desire.

2) PSC members must be spiritually mature and have depth in biblical training. They should not be new Christians.

People who have recently come to Christ are like babes. They are learning to take small steps, while feeding on the milk of the Word. Even if this new convert is an adult who is an educator, or gifted in business, this should not be mistaken for spiritual maturity or depth.

3) PSC members should have a good grasp of what the Bible says about the person and work of the pastor. Every member should familiarize themselves with what the New Testament has to say regarding the work and ministry of the Pastor. It is becoming more common to hear search committee members say something like, "well he doesn't have to be able to preach all that well.......... as long as he ministers to the church". Basically, this committee is looking for a hired hospital visitor, referee, and activity organizer that will do a good job in the area of public relations. Brethren, the Bible says that the pastors *number one* responsibility is to "preach the Word" (2nd Timothy 4:2)! His *second* responsibility is to prayerfully and intentionally train and equip <u>the church </u>to do the work of ministry and to come to maturity (Ephesians 4:11-16).

4) PSC members must have a working knowledge of fundamental Bible doctrines. After all, you are seeking someone to preach sound doctrine. The committee member should have clear understanding of the doctrine of salvation as well as the basic doctrines of the church.

5) PSC members of the team must be just that—team players. They must be respected by the congregation and by one another. These people should have patience and be able to work in harmony with others. These individuals should not make negative comments in front of other church members regarding committee members or the specifics of the search.

6) PSC members must be faithful church attenders, givers, and dedicated workers. More often than not, these will be the people who will work closely with the new pastor. They are also the kind of people the congregation will trust to do their best in searching for and recommending a pastor.

7) PSC members must be excellent listeners. You must not appoint people who only hear the prospective pastor speak but do not listen. They must be active listeners who not only hear what he *does say* but also realizes what he *doesn't say.* Sometimes the news is not in what he says, but it is in what he isn't saying.(My wife is excellent at active listening)!

8) PSC members should represent a cross-section of the families within the church family. If you choose to have five members on your search team, they should not be immediate family members. (Example: husband-wife/parent-child/siblings) Choosing members from five different immediate families will help to foster a unified spirit from the beginning.

Preliminary Organization

After the PSC has been selected and approved by a vote of the church, committee members should elect their own chairman. The chairman's duties will consist of calling the meetings and delegating duties as they arise. The chairman's vote and voice carries no more weight than any other members. The chairman will simply help to organize the process and be a spokesman for the committee.

Remember, the search for a pastor is usually a marathon, not a sprint. Spend a lot of time in prayer together. Keep the PSC on the church's prayer list. Stay close to one another spiritually, because the devil will wreak havoc within a divided group.

Chapter 4

The Posture of the Church During the Search

A friend of mine attends a church that went without a pastor for quite some time. When he spoke to me, their PSC had not reported to the congregation in months. He was concerned about the slow decrease in attendance and the overall mood of the church. They had called an Interim Pastor but things were just not going well. He and his wife were even considering visiting another church. I encouraged him to be patient for a little while longer to give their search committee the benefit of the doubt. They prayerfully stuck it out and today are very glad they did. God sent them an anointed pastor, and their church is truly being blessed.

I fully understand the frustration of a church in the dark. After all, we want to know what's going on! This the day of communication and information. We can email, text, twitter, instant message, spill it on My Space or file it on Facebook. So why can't we get a little information from our PSC?

It is a fact that the majority of church members will never serve on a search committee. You should thank the Lord for that! One of the brethren who served on the committee that presented me to the church I currently pastor remarked recently, "I'll never serve on another search committee." Talk about letting the air out of a pastor! Then he recovered by saying, "it had nothing to do with you pastor, just the difficulty of the task."

I am afraid there are many people who share my brother's sentiment about serving on a search committee more than once. The average church member has no idea of the degree of difficulty involved in finding a pastor for a full time *or* bi-vocational position.

Several years ago, a church in our area had an interesting time searching for a pastor. They received and reviewed over 300 resumes! Can you imagine? They saw the impressive, the imposter and the impossible. There were preachers who were in trouble with the law, convicted sex offenders, one supporting multiple living wives—you name it, they saw it.

The process was long and tough but they knew God's man for the hour was out there. They were right. God raised up a great servant for His church. He has enjoyed a wonderful ministry there and has been a tremendous asset to our local association of churches. I hope the Lord leaves him here for a long time.

Put yourself in the shoes of a member of that search committee. How would you like to face the same questions, not Sunday after Sunday, but service after service? People not serving on the committee, with no idea of the intensity of the task, often assume the committee is dragging its collective feet and that if they were really trying the mission should already have been accomplished.

Committee members are often peppered with questions: How much longer will this take? Are we getting close? How many preachers are you looking at? Why is this taking so long? We could have called three pastors by now! Church member, you need to take the advice of the younger generation and just chill out! Your committee needs your concern and your prayer, but not your criticism or added pressure.

Many congregations are like children in the back seat of an automobile, headed for a vacation. They are not interested in the trip—only the destination, asking, "Are we there yet?" and "How much longer?"

Churches often fail to realize that God does not work according to our time schedule. Think about this; God took six days to create our world and its inhabitants. Couldn't He have done it all in one day? After all, He is God. The answer is: God does what he does, how He does it, at the speed He does it, because He always knows best.

You may need to remind the church that God is not just working on the church's side of the issue, but He is moving in the heart of the next pastor as well. Remember the tired cliché, "Good things *do* usually come to those who wait." Besides, most churches are healthy enough to withstand a period of time without a pastor. With a solid word from the IP (Interim Pastor) every week, ongoing teaching and training in Sunday school or discipleship classes, and fellowship and worship continuing as usual, all will be well until God's man for the church is found.

One final thing in regard to the posture of the church during the search period. If a member of the church discovers the identity of one or more of the final candidates the committee is considering, this could be a potential problem. To illustrate, let me use a personal experience.

Several years ago, our local association appointed a search committee to find a new Director of Missions (DOM). I was not a member of this committee. One day the search team met in the vacant DOM office to narrow down the search to two candidates. They exited the office after the meeting, not realizing that someone had left the resumes of the two finalists on a bookshelf.

The next day, I was in that same office, doing some associational work, and there they were! The names that had been kept confidential for months were right before my eyes! One of these names I had never heard, while the other *did not please me.* The cover letter was all I saw. It was written by a very influential person who was recommending this individual for the position.

At that moment I had to make a decision. Do I call up one of the search committee members and express my concern and disagreement, or do I allow the Lord to work through the search committee? Long story short, I chose the latter, and left it in the Lord's hands. I am glad that

I did. If I had run ahead of God, I could have messed things up. On the day of the interviews, God gave clear direction for *His* choice. After a long search, we now have a great DOM.

The point is this. If the church is privy to too much information, there is potential for real problems. In extreme cases, a church member might take it upon themselves to approach a potential candidate on their own. This will almost always prove to be disastrous. If the church has voted on a committee and empowered them to conduct the search for, and interviewing of applicants, then the church member *not on that committee* has overstepped their bounds.

That's why it is very important for the PSC to be discreet in its work and careful with the information they handle. This is for the benefit of the candidate as well as the church. The church needs to be kept up to speed on the generalities of the search, but the names and personal information of potential candidates must be held privately by the committee. This is to protect everyone involved.

Chapter 5

The Selection Process

The process of turning dozens of referrals and resumes into the calling of a pastor can be very tedious and time consuming. The average time it takes to call a pastor is somewhere in the range of 9-16 months. I cannot stress how important it will be for everyone in the congregation to pray and seek the will of God throughout the lengthy process.

The church as a whole should lift up the PSC (Pastor Search Committee) to the Lord every day. It is important for the committee and the church to be in unity. At the outset, it is important that the PSC knows the methods and ground rules they will use to accomplish their goal.

The following method has been proven to be successful. Though there must be some flexibility to your method because unexpected events will arise during the search, there must be an overall structure in place to guide PSC members in a common direction.

Before you can begin the selection process, the chairman should call an initial meeting that involves every PSC member. **This first meeting should not be held unless every member can be present for the entire meeting.** (Tip: One member of the committee should act as secretary, taking notes on the main business of each meeting.) At this meeting the groundwork must be laid for receiving the names and qualifications of candidates. Pray about adopting something similar to this plan:

Step 1: Determine the qualifications for the new pastor.

Here are some recommended qualifications.

1. Experience

There are some churches who will consider candidates that have had no prior pastoral experience. All pastors must get their start somewhere. However, there are some churches that will need an experienced pastor. Every pastor cannot deal with the character, activity, demands, and personality of every church. The numerical size and spiritual condition of your membership are factors to consider when determining the experience you will require in a pastor. If you choose to require the candidate to have prior experience, how many years will be sufficient? Will experience as an associate pastor be considered?

2. *Education*

What will your educational requirements be? Decide if candidates should have a degree in one or more of the following: Theology, Divinity, Languages, or Ministry. What level of degree should they have? Will you require Bachelor, Masters, or Doctoral degrees?

Some churches do not require that a candidate have a degree if his experience in ministry makes up for it. This is one of the areas of allowed flexibility that should be given to the PSC. Personally, I have known many great pastors and powerful preachers who had *no* seminary or Bible school training. An anointing of the Holy Spirit cannot be replaced by intellectual education. When you find a man who has been "God called" first and *then* committed himself to a Biblical education for the glory of God, this what you look for regarding education.

3. Additional

Experience and education are foremost, but if there are any other requirements or preferences considered non-negotiable, this is the time to declare them.

For example, are you a traditional or contemporary congregation looking for a like-minded pastor? Do you have a doctrinal statement you want to share? How important is missions to your congregation? Does your church use only the King James Version of the Bible? Due to the varied interpretations of the qualifications for the office of a Bishop (pastor), there may be something your church wants stressed up front. For example, do you interpret "the husband of one wife" to mean *one living wife* or *one wife at a time?* These are issues that need to be decided ahead of time.

Is the PSC agreed on the spiritual, social, and marital status they will expect in a pastor? Add these to your list of requirements. This will save you and the candidates both time and trouble.

Several years ago, as a pastoral candidate, I met with a PSC from a church in our state. This church participated in an activity in which it would have been difficult for me to be involved. This opened the discussion into other areas. After our discussion, it was clear from the somber faces, that our personalities were very different, and that this would not be a likely marriage. Talks ended a few weeks later as I was not a "fit" for them.

If you have *anything* that is non-negotiable you should cover this early in the interview process, if not up front, as an additional requirement.

Step 2: Decide how and for how long you will gather applicants for the opening.

Here are some suggestions.

1. Referrals from other respected pastors.

No one knows preachers better than other preachers. It is a fact that many churches have called a pastor based primarily on a referral from another minister. Never do this instead of doing your own investigation of the candidate. Even other pastors can be misinformed occasionally.

2. Resumes from your association or organizational office (if available).

This seems to be the most popular choice for learning of candidates. Just remember that anyone can put anything in a resume.

3. Run an advertisement in your organizational publications.

The ad should contain the major requirements for the position: Full or part time, required education and degree, specific experience, and so on. (Appendix B)

4. Advertise your opening on internet sites.

Simply go to Google and type in "Pastor Jobs". There will be numerous links to many sites where you can list your opening. Have your requirements listed and choose an email address to which interested parties can send resumes. Normally this would be the church's email address, though it could also be the address of the chairman or another committee member. It might even be better for you to set up a temporary website that the interested parties can go to and correspond through.

5. Set a future date to stop receiving names and applicants.

There must be a point when you stop adding new names and begin to work with what you have. A period of 60 days should be sufficient to gather names and applicants. If you fail to receive an adequate number of inquiries or have not found a viable candidate, you can always advertise again.

Step 3: Review what your church by-laws or constitution requires for voting eligibility.

Most churches have these. For example, some congregations require a prospective pastor to receive a 90% "Yes" vote in order to be called as pastor. If you do not have any parameters set up for the voting process, I *strongly* suggest you create them. (Simply review those of other churches).

Do you allow *every* member of the church to vote on a pastor—even long inactive "members"? Many times, especially in rural churches, a crowd of inactive members will show up for a pastoral vote, often voting down a man of

God presented to the church by the PSC. It is interesting that some folks are not able to attend church for worship but are able to attend when there's a vote.

It would almost be comical if the stakes were not so serious. There are people (used of the devil), who have no honor, of lowly character, who think nothing of interjecting their carnal, fleshly influence into the vote on a pastor. **This is simple to prevent.**

During a business meeting of the church, simply prepare a motion that says, "in order to vote on a prospective pastor, an individual must have attended 50% or more of the services and church business meetings over the past 12 months. Make sure this is done at the beginning of your search, so as to not be a surprise at the last minute.

Some congregations take it one step further. Every so often they will "purge" their membership role of any able bodied person(s) who do not attend regularly. This may or may not be your preferred method but you do need to deal with this issue before you get too far into your next search.

A Guideline for the Process

After the advertising period is over, it is time to begin your work as a committee. The following steps are only suggestions and can be adjusted to meet the needs of your church.

Step 1

Make copies of each resume and inquiry. Give every PSC member a copy of each one. Allow three weeks to prayerfully review them. Pray that God will give each member direction and discernment. Each member should bring their top 25% of the resumes to the next meeting.

For example, if you receive 80 resumes, each members should select the top 20 candidates they feel best about. (We will continue using this number for the sake of illustration. You may determine a different number works better for you.) Keep *all* resumes for possible future use.

Step 2

At this meeting, members should compare their top 20 candidates, seeking a common thread. Compare the chosen names each member has brought. Also, consider the discussion of late referrals or hand- delivered resumes if allowed by your pre-established process guidelines.

Do not reduce the number of candidates at this meeting. This is a meeting for comparison and prayer. Take another 2 or 3 weeks to pray over these candidates, charging each committee member to narrow their 20 top candidate resumes down to 10 each feels best about.

Important: Remember to keep the church informed of your progress. This would be a good time to announce at the end of a Sunday morning service that you have a number of candidates and are narrowing the search. Remind the congregation to pray during this crucial time.

Step 3

Another meeting of the PSC should be held, with each member bringing the ten resumes they feel best about. Look again for that common thread of agreement among committee members. *Do not contact references yet.* That time will come soon.

You will not all bring the same ten resumes to this meeting, but you should narrow the search to ten that you can all agree on. If you are ready, get sermon recordings from each of your ten remaining candidates, on either CD or DVD. Pass these around until each member has heard every sermon. Technology is a great way to keep "miles" off of the committee.

Take the next two or three weeks to listen to the sermons. Remember, you are not trying to find a carbon copy of your departed pastor, but you are listening for doctrine, practical application, and conviction. Job one for a pastor is to "preach the Word." While listening to these messages, try narrowing your number to five candidates. **If this step takes longer, do not feel pressured; this is too important to rush.**

Candidates sometime change their mind when asked for a recording. One or more of the ten may choose to exit the process at this point.

Step 4

You should now get ready to conduct your first interviews with the five ministers you are most seriously considering to be the next pastor of your church. I suggest you do not attempt to meet with all five of these men in person. That would take too much time and involve too much travel. Set up a brief phone interview in which the PSC gathers around a speaker phone and speaks to the candidate. With today's cell phone technology you can meet just about anywhere. If possible you may be able to interview over videophone or even Skype. This interview is intended for the two parties to meet and get acquainted. Prepare a few questions that are designed to help you get to know the candidate a little better (Appendix C).

Step5

At this session you should narrow candidates down to two or three people to focus on. Team members should approach this meeting even more prayerfully than before. Our enemy would like nothing better than to derail you and your search at this point.

It is possible that there will be one candidate that seems to be in the front of every members mind, but don't stop the process just yet. You should have already heard these two or three men preach by CD or DVD. But there is nothing like being there in person. I know it is time-consuming, and it could be costly, but you need to have a face-to-face meeting with your top two (if not three) candidates and hear them preach in a service as well.

Step 5

All or part of the committee must hear each of the remaining candidates preach in a service. This may take several weeks to accomplish. Contact the candidates, letting them know that your PSC would like to meet them and hear them in person. There is usually a pastor friend who will let these candidates preach in a service at his church. Sometimes the candidate will be preaching in a revival nearby. Regardless of how you do it, you need to be in service with this person in a way that will not alert his church. Follow this same practice for a candidate who is not currently pastoring a church.

Resist the idea of letting any candidate preach at your church at this point. You do not want your entire church to hear anyone except the person whom the committee will recommend to the church.

This is another good time to update the church on your progress. Tell them you are in the process of traveling to hear someone and hopefully you will make a recommendation within a few weeks.

This is another point where it is possible that one or more of the candidates could choose to exit the process. With that in mind, **do not show up at the candidate's church where he pastors**. In every way, keep his interest in your church confidential.

Step 6

After the committee hears the remaining candidates preach, they should meet and discuss the direction they feel led to go. It is possible that one, two, or all three ministers still rate highly in the minds of the PSC. This is the time to begin researching these individuals in depth. Without a doubt, the committee is at its most critical point in the search.

A background check is recommended for any candidate with whom the committee is not fully acquainted. There are many agencies that will provide this service for a fee. Go to www.Intelius.com and they will provide a criminal background check for the fee of $49.95. There is also an organization called "Infocheck USA" that performs basically the same service. Such checks are worth every penny and can help the committee to avoid a terrible mistake! As I said before, anyone can type *anything* on a resume. Sometimes the big news is what they *didn't include*.

It is not just money issues that should concern us. Churches should be aware of any criminal record, outstanding warrants, bad debts and more. *There are also men in the world today that would be a danger to the children of the church. .*

Less than one week ago I saw a resume that had been sent to our area. I did not recognize the mans name or current membership but I did recognize the name of the last church he pastored. The dates of tenure were also shocking to me. Only through the help of the Lord did I remember that a pastor in recent years, from that church, was convicted on sexual abuse charges. The charges involved a little girl only 3 years old. **This mans resume listed no references from that particular church. No church can afford to be naïve in this day and age. Check them out!**

It is the duty of the PSC to research these individuals thoroughly. <u>All references</u> they provide should be contacted (Appendix D). Then go deeper. Go into the former church field if possible, and ask a few questions. Get a feel for how his community viewed him and felt about him. If it is too far for the entire committee to investigate, just send one or two people. Believe me friend; this is one step you cannot afford to omit.

A church in our area was disappointed to find out recently that their pastor had embezzled several thousand dollars over a period of time.

A properly conducted review of his past ministry and references could have uncovered the financial improprieties that arose at his previous church.

Some churches now require a credit check. I am not a fan of this, due to the fact that every individual should be afforded at least some measure of privacy. Let me suggest that you wait until you narrow your search to one or two candidates before requesting financial information. If you order a background check and do a *complete* check on all of his references, you may be able to skip this task.

On my personal resume, I have the name and number of my Loan Officer along with the name of the financial institution I bank with. The officer has written permission from me to discuss my status as a customer as it pertains to financial stability. No amounts are to be discussed. Only that

I am a long time customer who is current with all loans. If that is not enough, I *would* allow a committee to do a credit check if I knew beyond a shadow of a doubt that God was calling me there.

If you feel the need for a credit check, make it the last order of business. By this time your committee should realize it is approaching the time when they must vote for one person.

Step 7

After much prayer and patience, if one candidate has not become a clear favorite, you must now call for a vote. ***Remember, you agreed that the majority would rule and that you would do what is necessary to be in unity with the rest of the committee.*** The goal for this committee session should be to come out with clear unity behind one candidate to interview and subsequently present to the church.

Step 8

After the vote is taken, the committee should meet with the remaining candidate for a question and answer session. You should inform him that, as a committee, God has brought the process to this point—and that there is no other candidate being interviewed. He should also know that, if the meeting and interview goes well and God continues to lead the search team to do so, it is your intention to reveal his name to the church and secure a date for him to preach in view of a call to pastor your church.

You could invite his wife to sit in on the interview if you would like to meet her and get a feel for how they interact with each other. This session should involve a discussion that answers questions for both parties (Appendix E). You ***should not*** go into this interview without at least an outline of the meeting. The entire committee should know what is to be asked and discussed in this interview.

The church should ask questions about:
1. His salvation experience, call to ministry and ordination.
2. Doctrine—the single most important issue.
3. Pastoral philosophy—how he intends to lead the church.
4. Family situation—get a feel for the husband/wife relationship. Also to meet the children if you so desire.
5. What the candidate expects from the church in regards to his authority over the pulpit, his relationship with the deacons, and the response to his leadership he hopes to receive.

The church should provide information regarding:

1. What it expects from its pastor.

2. The direction it desires to go.

3. Housing

4. Salary and benefits

** If this meeting goes as well and the committee agrees this is the man your church needs, the chairman should contact the candidate within a couple of days and a date should be set for him to preach in view of a call to pastor before the entire congregation.

Step 9

This should be a meeting between the PSC and the church where the final candidate is recommended as the pastor. The committee should explain how they came to their decision and declare their unity in this matter. The name of the candidate should be revealed, along with information that will give the congregation an idea of what he is like. The church should know the date he is coming to preach well in advance. You should also remind everyone of the voting guidelines and the percentage that is needed to call a pastor as well as the *requirement of recent attendance* in order to be eligible to vote. Again, this requirement will help prevent Satan from causing confusion.

Step 10

The Sunday has come for the candidate to preach. If possible, you should have a fellowship meal after the service(s) to let the church body get to know him and his family better. Following this, I recommend that the church spend at least one more week in prayer before you vote. I also recommend that the PSC talk to a few members of the church to get an idea of how they received the candidate and to pass on more information about the prospective pastor that may not have been shared in the Sunday service.

Just remember, *never* share any private information that you were privy to from the background/credit check.

Step 11

Congratulations! The day is finally here! You are prepared to vote on your prospective pastor. The vote should be conducted according to the church by-laws for calling a pastor. Committee members have served in a capacity that few ever will. They have sought the will of God in calling a pastor to one of His churches. I am sure there is a special reward for faithful search committee members who served in this vital task, for the glory of the Lord (and not to get his or her own way).

Important Things After the Search

1. You should never share resumes with another church or committee unless you receive express permission from the minister. This could cause a world of damage to him and to the cause of Christ. Ask before you share.
2. Any resumes that were not considered should be disposed of and all names should be kept confidential. This is one of the strictly confidential parts of your service.
3. If by some unforeseen reason, the church votes to reject the proposed candidate, you should try to understand the reason for the opposition. It is usually impossible to call for a second vote on the same candidate. A down vote indicates an underlying issue. Find it, deal with it, and decide the best point in the

process to restart the process of looking for a pastor.

Chapter 6

What is a Pastor?

Several years ago, my father-in-law and I were invited to an ordination service to help ordain a friend of ours into the ministry. One of the messages that day was delivered by an elderly pastor from the area. He began the message by asking: "What is a pastor?" There are many possible answers to this questions. The accuracy of these many answers should be tested by the sections of the Bible that deal with pastors. The elderly pastor went on to say, "Brethren, always remember this—Elder is the man, Bishop is the office, and Pastor is the work".

This has always been the simplest yet most detailed answer that I have ever heard to the question about this position within the church. These are the three Scriptural lenses through which every pastor should be viewed. All that is said regarding this man in the scripture can be gathered under the canopy of these three titles: Elder, Bishop, Pastor. The reason for this is due to the fact that there are three Greek words used interchangeably throughout the New Testament to describe the New Testament Minister.

As an Elder (or Presbyter)—the minister should be given respect and honor as a man and servant of God. Biblically, he is to receive "double honor." The minister/pastor should be held in esteem for the sake of his office as he is a Bishop. God's Word instructs us that this man should never be a novice or beginner concerning spiritual things. On the contrary, he should be a person of integrity, wisdom and spiritual stature.

The Elder is not set up as a *lord* over the church but as a *leader* within the church. Eldership rule in a church is not Scriptural, it is dictatorial. Only Christ is the head of the Church and the elder is to be an undershepherd to it. He should lead with the heart and mind of Christ.

The congregation has the final vote or say in matters of choice and action. It is the Elder's responsibility to inform and lead them in the ways of God. The Elder should never be accused of any wrongdoing without actual proof or without the presence of two or three witnesses. Refuse to participate in gossip sessions that assassinate the character and reputation of your pastor.

As a Bishop (Overseer)—your pastor occupies one of only two biblical offices. The other office is that of a Deacon. The man that desires the office of Bishop desires a "good work" (1 Timothy 3:1). He must meet God's express qualifications for the job. His reputation must be one of good standing with the saved and the lost. His home life and marriage must be consistent with God's desires and designs. He is to be a person with self -control in all areas. *These qualifications are not just good ideas; they are a must* (1 Timothy 3:2-7).

This office comes with many responsibilities, but it also comes with many trials and temptations. The Bishop should never be immature or a babe in Christ. Even if he is inexperienced as a pastor, he should be experienced in the Word and disciplined in his study. As far as I am concerned, it is the highest office in the land and should be held up as such.

As your Pastor (Shepherd)—he must be all of these things and more. There is no way to say all of the things that I *could say* in this space. Let me simply lay out one of the best passages from the Bible to describe the heart and duties of the Pastor.

The passage contains the words of Paul in Acts 20, as he stops at Mellitus and calls for the elders of the church at Ephesus to come and meet with him one last time. Paul had pastored in Ephesus for over 3 years and had a special heart toward the people there. I would like to highlight some characteristics of Paul's ministry to these people. These are the same characteristics a church should desire in a pastor.

See Acts 20: 17-18.

[17]And from Mellitus he sent to Ephesus, and called the elders of the church.

[18]And when they were come to him, he said unto them, Ye know, from the first day that I came into Asia, after what manner I have been with you at all seasons,

#1 Persistence—Paul started well, ran well, and finished well there. He preached and served *in* season, *out* of season and *at all* seasons. He would not quit or be stalled. Every church should want a pastor who exhibits the care of a good shepherd and not the cowardice of a hireling.

See Acts 20:19.

[19]Serving the LORD with all humility of mind, and with many tears, and temptations, which befell me by the lying in wait of the Jews:

#2 Passion—Only a love for Christ and His people will create this kind of passionate service. Paul pastored all people with lowliness of mind. He wept with tenderness and compassion for the saved as well as the unsaved. He served with a purposeful, willing heart, even when he was attacked by unsaved religionists. Few men will ever know the challenges that their pastor faces as he attempts to minister to some people.

See Acts 20:20-21.

[20]And how I kept back nothing that was profitable unto you, but have shewed you, and have taught you publicly, and from house to house,

[21]Testifying both to the Jews, and also to the Greeks, repentance toward God, and faith toward our Lord Jesus Christ.

#3 Plain—As a preacher, Paul painted a word picture that was simple and clear. No flowery speech or impressive vocabulary was needed. He presented Christ and Him crucified, to all peoples on their level. My father once told me, "Son, plain speech is not easily misunderstood."

See Acts 20:22-25.

²²And now, behold, I go bound in the spirit unto Jerusalem, not knowing the things that shall befall me there:

²³Save that the Holy Ghost witnesseth in every city, saying that bonds and afflictions abide me.

²⁴But none of these things move me, neither count I my life dear unto myself, so that I might finish my course with joy, and the ministry, which I have received of the Lord Jesus, to testify the gospel of the grace of God.

²⁵And now, behold, I know that ye all, among whom I have gone preaching the kingdom of God, shall see my face no more.

#4 Perception—A pastor does not do well, nor will he last long without some discernment. We cannot just stumble along without following the leadership of the Holy Spirit. These verses reveal Paul's perception of the ministry into which God had placed him.

The man of God always sees his ministry through the eyes of the Holy Spirit. He has the perception of not only how and why to minister, but also where and when to minister. Paul understood when to stay at Ephesus. He discerned the things God wanted him to do there. He also knew when it was time to move on, though he was saddened that this would be their last fellowship together this side of heaven. The apostle knew he must go to Jerusalem, regardless of what awaited him there.

See Acts 20:26-27.

[26]Wherefore I take you to record this day, that I am pure from the blood of all men.

[27]For I have not shunned to declare unto you all the counsel of God.

#5 Proclamation—Every pastor has been given the charge to preach the Word. He is to preach the whole Word—*all* the counsel of God. Your church has a right to expect the pastor to deal with all doctrines and subject matter in the volume of Scripture. The maturity of believers within the church is at stake. You do not want a back-patting, ear-tickling, apologizing compromiser in the pulpit. God expects his men to expound on all that He has written to his church.

This is how Paul could be free from the blood of all men. He had held back nothing that could be profitable to these believers.

See Acts 20:28-32.

[28]Take heed therefore unto yourselves, and to all the flock, over the which the Holy Ghost hath made you overseers, to feed the church of God, which he hath purchased with his own blood.

²⁹For I know this, that after my departing shall grievous wolves enter in among you, not sparing the flock.

³⁰Also of your own selves shall men arise, speaking perverse things, to draw away disciples after them.

³¹Therefore watch, and remember, that by the space of three years I ceased not to warn every one night and day with tears.

³²And now, brethren, I commend you to God, and to the word of his grace, which is able to build you up, and to give you an inheritance among all them which are sanctified.

#6 Preparation—The exiting Paul reminded the "preacher boys" that they would oversee the church now that he was leaving. He had prepared them to feed the church the Word of God. He also warned them of the attack of Satan that would undoubtedly come. They would be attacked from without as well as within.

He also taught them to live for God and to live for God's Word. The Word will edify and equip the saint. The minister should preach with the present and future of the church in heart and mind. He should be concerned about what happens while he is there and after he is long gone.

See Acts 20:33-35.

^{33}I have coveted no man's silver, or gold, or apparel.

^{34}Yea, ye yourselves know, that these hands have ministered unto my necessities, and to them that were with me.

^{35}I have shewed you all things, how that so labouring ye ought to support the weak, and to remember the words of the Lord Jesus, how he said, It is more blessed to give than to receive.

#7 Pattern—Paul was an example to the young church at Ephesus. This is the same advice that Paul gave to the young preacher Timothy. The pastor should live a practical, visible, and Spirit-filled life before his congregation.

How can a church have respect for a "do as I say" pastor? Before we are *pastors* we are *men*. We should live as a Christian man ought to live, being an example of the believer.

See Acts 20:36-38.

³⁶And when he had thus spoken, he kneeled down, and prayed with them all.

³⁷And they all wept sore, and fell on Paul's neck, and kissed him,

³⁸Sorrowing most of all for the words which he spake, that they should see his face no more. And they accompanied him unto the ship.

#8 Prayer—The power of the pulpit and the pew is found in prayer and communion with the

Father. Hundreds of times, Paul prayed with the Ephesians. Now in his departure, the last act of their beloved friend was to kneel in the sand and touch heaven on their behalf. This is the part of the pastor's life that is hardest to maintain. With the demands on his time and the necessity of study, it is easy to neglect prayer. The praying pastor will teach his congregation to pray.

These are just a few of the characteristics and qualities that should be evident in a pastor. Remember, this is a composite list. Men of God should develop these qualities as the years go by. There are no perfect pastors, just as there are no perfect churches. However, I do believe there are perfect "fits" when the right church and the right pastor come together.

In closing, I would like to present a serious charge given by an aged Paul to the young pastor, Timothy. It is a charge every pastor should take personally. This Scripture brings to a very specific light, the value of finding a sound, biblically fortified pastor for today's church.

We are in a time of immeasurable apathy and unparalleled apostasy. (Apostates are men who do not adhere to the doctrines of Christ, nor do they contend for the faith that was once delivered to the saints.) They are rising up everywhere around us as well as among us. Paul places a premium upon zeal for the truth and soundness of doctrine from the pulpit and so should you!

In Second Timothy 4, Paul said:

¹I charge thee therefore before God, and the Lord Jesus Christ, who shall judge the quick and the dead at his appearing and his kingdom;

²Preach the word; be instant in season, out of season; reprove, rebuke, exhort with all long suffering and doctrine.

³For the time will come when they will not endure sound doctrine; but after their own lusts shall they heap to themselves teachers, having itching ears;

⁴And they shall turn away their ears from the truth, and shall be turned unto fables.

⁵But watch thou in all things, endure afflictions, do the work of an evangelist, make full proof of thy ministry.

The man you are looking for should strive to meet this charge and see these things done within his own ministry.

I pray that God will bless you as you search for the man He has prepared. Accept nothing less than God's will for your church. It is my sincere hope that something in this book has helped you. And if it has, then to God be the Glory!

Brother Scott

[i] Dale Huff, *Mastering Transitions* (Preaching Point, Alabama State Board of Missions)

[ii] Richard A. Murphy, *Life-line for Pastors* (Maranatha Publications 2002)

[iii] William Shakespeare, *Romeo and Juliet* (Act 2 Scene 2)

Appendix A

Sample Interim Pastor Contract

_This document sets forth the intention of _____ _____ Church to call _____ as Interim Pastor. _____ Church has empowered a designated committee to extend this call, and to release, _____ at the appropriate time. As Interim Pastor, _____ _____, agrees to perform the following duties and services.

He will:
- Prepare and deliver sermons for Sunday morning, Sunday night and Wednesday night services.
- Maintain doctrinal integrity in his preaching and teaching.
- Have the responsibility to baptize new believers as authorized by the church.
- Perform the ministerial duties related to weddings, funerals, baby dedications, etc. etc.. (But only as requested)
- Be prepared to visit with those who become *seriously* ill, or are facing major surgery.

- Handle any necessary administrative duties that must be kept current in the absence of a permanent pastor.

In exchange for his services, _____ Church agrees to pay _____ _____ per week salary. (Note: The salary should be commensurate with the ministers duties and experience. He should also be reimbursed for any mileage and expenses he incurs while working for the church)

While serving as Interim Pastor, _____ agrees that he will not:
- Join _____ Church.
- Be considered for the vacant pastor position.
- Be involved in the search process for the new pastor.
- Moderate business meetings.
- Serve on any committee.

As Interim Pastor, _____ agrees that unless he is unable to fill the entire interim period, he will remain with the church until a permanent pastor can be called. If _____ must resign his position before a pastor can be called, he will give *no less* than a two week notice to the committee that called him.

_____   _____
Interim Pastor   Date   Interim Committee   Date
                                 Chairman

Appendix B

Senior Pastor

Calvary Christian Church is accepting resumes for the position of Senior Pastor. This is a full-time position. We are a church enjoying a blended style of praise and worship. We are a mission-minded congregation looking for Gods man to lead us into the future. The church is located just West of Augusta, Georgia on highway 19. This is a growing area with many opportunities for outreach and evangelism. Applicants should have prior pastoral experience. We ask that any respondent have at least a Bachelors degree in Ministry or Theology. Please send resumes to:

Calvary Christian Church
Attn: Pastor Search Committee
1755 Georgia Hwy 19
Hopewell, Ga. 22367
(or)
Fax your resume to: 1-234-567-8901 (Please send cover sheet)

Bi-vocational Pastor

The Carter Creek Baptist Church in Magnolia, Arkansas is receiving resumes for the position of Pastor. This is a Bi-vocational position. We are a church with a 150 year heritage. We are fudamentalist Baptists, using *only* the King James 1611 version of the Bible. Carter Creek is a member of the Spruce Pine Baptist association. Interested parties may send resumes to:

Carter Creek Baptist Church
P.O. Box 2212
Magnolia, Arkansas 65473
(or)
E-mail our Search Committee Chairman at;
Williamposey@youmail.com

Appendix C

Sample of Speaker-Phone Interview (With Conversation Guide)

* Contact the pastor who you wish to interview ahead of time so you may set up the following brief interview.

** After you reach the candidate and all committee members are present, remind everyone that this is simply a preliminary interview that does express your interest in Brother_____, but this in no way obligates either parties to go any further than this phone conversation.

*** The interview could follow a form similar to the one below.

1. Introduce each member by name and any position they hold in the church.
2. State that we have all reviewed the resume, listened to sermon(s), and agreed that we wanted to get to know you a little better.
3. Tell us a little about your childhood/school years and growing up.

4. What was your family like…..some of your favorite memories.
5. How did you meet your wife? Tell us about your children.
6. Share with us your testimony ……how you came to know the Lord.
7. Share with the committee your call to the ministry.
8. How has your family handled you being a pastor?
9. What do you enjoy most about your current (or last) church?
10. What led to you sending your resume to us?

**** End the conversation by thanking him for his time as well as the committee members for theirs. Also remind him that this was a preliminary interview. The committee will pray and seek Gods direction concerning a second contact. The candidate will receive a call to set up an interview in person **or** to let him know that the committee feels led to end the process here. Close with prayer for him and your church.

Appendix D

Sample Phone Interview for Calling References

Hello, my name is _____, and I am from _____ church. We are currently interviewing _____ in consideration of becoming our next pastor. Bro. _____ has listed you as a reference on his resume. Do you have a few minutes to discuss your relationship with Bro. _____? Great, then let me start by asking: 1. How you are familiar with Bro. _____?
2. His resume says_____. To the best of your knowledge, is that information correct?
3. In general, how did you/your church feel about Bro._____
4. To your knowledge, is there any reason our church should not consider Bro. _____ for pastor?

Mr./Mrs. _____, thank you for your time. I appreciate your help today.

* You should be aware that it is not uncommon for references to be people who either loved the candidate or really disliked him. Either way you should make notes of your conversation to report to the committee.

Appendix E

Suggestion Questions for Final Interview

These are just a few of the questions and topics that should be a part of this final interview with the candidate. There is also a list of a few items that need to be shared with the candidate.

Questions and Topics

1. Please share with the committee your salvation experience, call to ministry, ordination and a brief summary of your ministry experience up to the present. Including any Biblical training or education you have received.
2. What are your convictions regarding the Bible and its truths? Is it Gods Word? Do you accept that it is inspired, inerrant, infallible and indestructible? How do you feel about missions and evangelism?
3. Doctrine is important to us. Please share what *you believe* to be process God uses to save a lost individual. In short, can you tell us how you explain

justification. (This would be a good place to ask any other major doctrinal questions that you need answered)
4. What is your Idea of a healthy church.
5. Please discuss your expectations of the deacons/teachers of the church you pastor.
6. What do you see as your strengths/weaknesses as a pastor.
7. We're sure you already know a few things about our congregation or you would not have gone this far in the process. Tell us why you will be leaving your present church and what is drawing you to us.
8. Share with us something you initiated in a former ministry that has worked well. Is there anything that did not work well and how would you approach it next time?
9. Is your wife and children completely on board with you in this ministry.
10. In Ephesians 4:11-16 the Bible teaches that you have been specifically gifted for ministry, by God, to help mature, train and unify His people. Colossians 1:28 says that you are to "warn every man and teach every man in all wisdom" in order to present every man "perfect in Christ". What do these verses mean to you and how would you accomplish this in our congregation?
11. Is there *anything* not included on your resume that this committee should know about you before we go any further in this process?

* The following information should be shared with the prospective pastor at this point. You should have the financial information typed up or in a small packet that can be given to the candidate to take with him.

- A brief history of the church including a current directory (if available)
- What this church expects from a pastor
- Salary Information
- Benefits such as Insurance/retirement
- Allowances such as housing/car or gas/pulpit materials
- Vacation time
- Time off for Missions work/conference attendance/ revivals

Any other financial or practical information you deem important.

* The candidate should be given the opportunity to ask any remaining questions. The meeting should close with prayer for a clear direction from God and for the will of God to be done in the life of the candidate as well as the church.

CPSIA information can be obtained
at www.ICGtesting.com
Printed in the USA
FFHW011115260819
54573920-60251FF